CYBER ATTACKS, COUNTERATTACKS, AND ESPIONAGE

spyware

p

spam

h

i
s
h
i
n
g

date
security

virus alert!

virus detected

CYBER ATTACKS, COUNTERATTACKS, AND ESPIONAGE

malware

v
i
r
u
s

a
t
t
a
c
k

25%

30%

DANIEL E. HARMON

ROSEN
PUBLISHING

Published in 2017 by The Rosen Publishing Group, Inc.
29 East 21st Street, New York, NY 10010

First Edition

Library of Congress Cataloging-in-Publication Data

Names: Harmon, Daniel E., author.
Title: Cyber attacks, counterattacks, and espionage / Daniel E. Harmon.
Description: First edition. | New York : Rosen Publishing, 2017. | Series:
  Cryptography: code making and code breaking | Includes bibliographical
  references and index.
Identifiers: LCCN 2016018413 | ISBN 9781508173168 (library bound)
Subjects: LCSH: Cyberterrorism—Juvenile literature. | Computer
  crimes—Juvenile literature. | Espionage—Juvenile literature.
Classification: LCC HV6773.15.C97 H37 2017 | DDC 364.16/8—dc23
LC record available at https://lccn.loc.gov/2016018413

Manufactured in China

CONTENTS

INTRODUCTION

Millions of Americans with health insurance policies were shocked in February 2015 by news that the medical database of one of the nation's largest insurers was infiltrated by hackers. Anthem revealed that cyber invaders had broken into its computer servers. Records of almost 80 million people were accessed. They contained personal information such as Social Security numbers, birthdays, physical addresses, email addresses, and employment data.

The breach did not occur overnight. The hemorrhage of information probably occurred over a period of weeks, investigators

The Anthem website is displayed on a computer screen in 2015, shortly after it was disclosed that the medical database of the major insurance corporation had been hacked.

believe, during December 2014. Anthem's information technology (IT) department learned of it in January. Information industry observers expect the personal data has been exchanged on the cyber criminal black market, and it could lead to incidents of identity theft for years to come. Even the short-term losses were enormous. It cost Anthem millions of dollars just to notify customers and advise them about monitoring their insurance accounts.

Some cybersecurity analysts suspect the attack was the work of hackers in China, possibly operating with or for that country's government. Foreign agencies are interested in obtaining personal data about government employees and contractors—particularly in the area of national defense. Intelligence professionals worry that hacks of health-related companies may be part of foreign governments' espionage strategies. International espionage is one of the oldest practices of deception in the world, and its agents now have a powerful new tool: digital technology.

Whoever the culprits and whatever their motives, the Anthem data breach is among the worst experienced by corporations in the digital era. Disturbingly, similar events are becoming all too commonplace. Before the Anthem calamity, companies such as JPMorgan Chase, eBay, Target, Neiman Marcus, and Home Depot lost information to hackers.

An important issue that has arisen in recent years, especially after the Anthem episode, is that of data encryption regulations. Many corporations take it upon themselves to encrypt customer data. Federal and state governments have passed related laws but have arrived at no uniform guidelines.

Cybercrime is a modern-day extension of a centuries-old routine. Organizations and individuals—including government agencies and political leaders—encrypt, or code, top-secret and delicate messages before sending them. Criminals and criminal agencies contrive to break the codes and exploit the secret information. Over time, cryptography has progressed from visual signals and pen-and-ink codes to mechanical cipher systems to digital encryption and decryption.

Cryptography is the science—and, in a sense, also the art—of coding. The term "cryptography" can be interpreted from early Greek language as "secret writing." A system is devised in which a transmitted message is enciphered or "scrambled" so that it can be understood only by the sender and recipient. To anyone who intercepts it, the message makes no sense. The sender and recipient know the "key" for coding (locking) and decoding (unlocking) the altered phonetic alphabet that is used to craft the message.

In basic ways, cryptography in the Internet age is similar to criminal and crime-fighting cryptography systems used for hundreds of years by deviants and police. Computer hacking now is carried out at local, corporate, and international levels. Law enforcement specialists in those realms use much the same computer technology as criminals use, tracking down the criminals.

CHAPTER 1

A NEW VARIATION OF CRYPTOGRAPHY

The art and science of cryptography has come a long way. As always, it continues to play a complex role in crime and international espionage today. It also is a weapon of warfare. However, the types of crime, spying, and warfare for which it is used now are extraordinarily different from those of the past.

Codes were used in ancient times to send private messages. Julius Caesar (100–44 BCE) employed a code in which each letter of a word was advanced three places forward. The letter A became D; S became V, and so on.

There are two basic types of ciphers. One type uses the transposition of letters in a word to make it unrecognizable at first glance. A simple transposition technique is reversal. The word "think" would be ciphered as "kniht." The word "glowing" would be "gniwolg."

The other type of cipher is substitution. Again, a simple example is replacing

Cryptography has a long, rich history. Roman general Julius Caesar used a secret code 2,000 years ago.

PASSWORDS: BASIC CYBERSECURITY SAFEGUARDS

Practically everyone who uses the Internet understands that their computer's operating system, Internet service provider, social networks, shopping and auction sites, and other frequently visited places require passwords. Passwords ensure the person at the keyboard is the person who truly is authorized to use those systems.

The use of passwords is an ancient security technique. For example, it was a way to verify that a military messenger moving from one army encampment to another was a friendly courier, not an enemy spy. If upon arrival the messenger could

Using strong passwords is a basic deterrent to cyber attacks. Still, hackers often manage to decode them with sophisticated hacking technology.

state the prearranged password, all was okay. If not, the messenger would be arrested or killed on sight.

Computer passwords today serve basically the same purpose. They are keys for gaining entry. For that reason, they are of obvious interest to hackers. A deciphered password can be a ticket for a cyber intruder to steal a valuable store of data.

Passwords are a form of cryptography. A digital password is a string of keyboard characters composed by the computer user. Computer manufacturers and digital service providers urge users to come up with strong passwords. Too frequently, people spend only seconds thinking up passwords that will be easy for them to remember—and easy for hackers to decipher. For instance, consumers might use their middle name spelled backward, a pet's name, or a favorite food as a password. Savvy hackers with automated tools who target their accounts and explore their online presence can detect such simplistic passwords in minutes or seconds.

In large companies and professional firms, information technology (IT) experts insist that employees use strong passwords for accessing company files and going online. Moreover, they want employees to change their passwords regularly—daily or weekly, in some organizations. This makes it far more difficult for a hacker to break into the company's computer system by stealing an employee's computer identity.

alphabetic letters with numerals: 1 for A, 2 for B, 3 for C, etc. Thus, the word "band" would be represented by the numbers 2, 1, 14, and 4.

The previous examples of traditional codes are extremely simplistic. Cyber coding today is amazingly complex. It cannot be enciphered or deciphered without computers.

CYBERSECURITY TECHNOLOGY

Most information that exists today is available and distributed in digital formats. Much of it can be found freely on the Internet by anyone.

Certain digital information files are not available for everyone to access on the Internet. They are stored on private computers. These include classified government documents, including top-secret military information; closely guarded company patent, financial, and marketing data; people's medical and financial records; and individuals' personal or private details. Only Internet users who have authorization can download them from the information providers' websites or internal computer systems. The owner or provider of the information does not want this confidential information to be accessible to the public at large.

To keep the data from prying eyes, information security specialists use different technology tools to encrypt/decrypt the data and to block intruders. Techniques include using digital signatures and digital fingerprints, speech verification, computer system firewalls, and anti-malware programs. Disturbingly, hackers have connived ways to break into heavily guarded stores of confidential digital information.

NEW TOOLS FOR AN OLD CRIME

Computer hacking has given new meaning to an age-old category of criminal practice: espionage. Espionage is the theft of secret, protected information or intelligence. The information may be held by governments, businesses, or ordinary people. Certain entities and individuals who are not authorized to have the information employ espionage agents, or spies, to stealthily obtain it for them.

Espionage has been a fascinating area of criminology for many centuries. In most scenarios, the actual gathering of the secret intelligence is only one part of an elaborate strategy. Criminologists identify five steps in the typical espionage operation:

1. Determine exactly what information is desired and where it is stored.
2. Have agents (now including cyber hackers) obtain the information.
3. Examine and organize the collected information.
4. Present the organized intelligence to the mastermind (decision maker) who initiated the operation.
5. Decide whether to use the information and, if so, how to use it most effectively.

Until the era of modern communications, espionage agents were confined to working on the ground. Army commanders sent scouts to investigate the positions and numbers of opposing forces. Spies entered enemy camps, pretending to be allies. In political espionage, individuals who appeared to be ordinary citizens, above suspicion, befriended and became intimate with government officials. Some of the professional spies hired by governments operated so brilliantly that their enemies did not realize their intelligence gathering until years after the leaked information had done its damage.

Cyber espionage is practiced by governments against other governments, corporations against rival corporations, and crime syndicates against the business world at large. It also is practiced at the domestic level—people who seek to impersonate, threaten, or ruin the reputations of individuals they dislike. In some ways, the tactics used in cyber espionage are similar to those used in ages past—for example, gaining the confidence of the targeted victim. In the Internet age, even a child who is skilled in computer use and online manipulation can engage in what amounts to espionage, extracting confidential information about individuals or organizations. Today, hacking and international, corporate, and domestic espionage go hand in hand.

A THREAT SPREADS GLOBALLY ONLINE

The Internet has facilitated the work of information hackers and introduced an alarming new dimension to the subject of cryptography. Online services as well as companies, organizations, and government agencies that function on the Internet use powerful security technology to protect their digital assets. Practical individuals use strong passwords and take advantage of firewalls and anti-malware programs to protect themselves.

Nevertheless, breaches have become inevitable. Clever, relentless hackers find ways through the cyber walls constructed by security software engineers. Targets range from children to major corporations and federal government agencies. Examples of recent cyber attacks include the following.

CORPORATIONS AND BUSINESSES

Dozens of major companies and thousands of smaller businesses have suffered breaches of their confidential records. Apple systems have been hit more than once. The Target retail chain had an estimated 40 million customers' financial data breached during the 2013 Christmas shopping season. Customers filed a class action lawsuit. In a 2015 court settlement, Target agreed to pay $10 million to affected customers and to upgrade its data security procedures.

Target, one of the largest discount retailers in the United States, has been one of numerous major companies victimized by cyber criminals.

A cyber attack on Sony Corporation in December 2014 disrupted its PlayStation entertainment network. Hackers demanded that Sony stop showing a new comedy film, *The Interview*, which the hackers claimed was a "movie of terrorism."

Stephen Cobb, in a 2015 post at the welivesecurity.com international security website, reflected, "Theft in cyberspace can be performed on a scale not possible in meatspace. The folks who stole payment card data from Target in 2013 were able to pocket, in a matter of months, a lot more money than all the bank robbers in America that year (some of whom were shot and killed in the act)."

One category of business targeted by hackers is particularly unsettling: hospitals. In February 2016, a medical center in California paid a ransom equaling $17,000 in Bitcoins to intruders who literally held its computer system hostage. A hospital employee apparently opened an attachment to what appeared to be a routine financial email statement. The opened file installed cyber code that locked up the computer system. The hospital administration decided the quickest way to regain control was to pay the criminals the ransom they demanded for the decryption key.

Technologists agreed that paying the ransom probably was the fastest way for the hospital staff to resolve the crisis. The solution raised concerns, though, that the incident would further embolden "computer-nappers." It could lead to an increase in expanded assaults against soft target (easy to breach) organizations.

By confiscating the hospital's data, skeptics added, the criminals potentially disrupted critical health care services. Those included access by doctors and surgeons to important patient information and the monitoring of patients' mobile medical devices.

GOVERNMENT AGENCIES

The White House, US State Department, US Postal Service, and National Atmospheric and Oceanic Administration are among the federal government institutions that have been breached by hackers. Chinese agents, possibly working for the Chinese government, are suspected.

Other government hacking targets have been the US Office of Personnel Management, which maintains information about government officials who have top-secret credentials, and US Investigations Services, a government contractor. An outside computer technician confessed to stealing records from US Coast Guard computers that were brought to him for repair.

Hackers have stolen data from all kinds of government entities, including the White House in Washington, DC.

State government agencies have been hacked as well. The following is just one of many examples: Foreign agents obtained the Social Security numbers of 3.6 million South Carolina citizens who filed their income tax returns with the state department of revenue between 1998 and 2012.

ONLINE SERVICES AND SOCIAL MEDIA SITES

In May 2014, the online auction site eBay informed its customers they all needed to change their passwords. The reason: Several months earlier, eBay discovered, its customer database had been hacked. Stolen were usernames, passwords, phone numbers, and other personal details. Claiming responsibility for the eBay hack was the Syrian Electronic Army, a politically motivated hacker group established to support Bashar al-Assad, the president of Syria. They gained entrance to the database after stealing the login credentials of certain eBay employees. Approximately two months went by before the company found out that the confidential employee data had been pilfered.

Only a month before the eBay news broke, AOL acknowledged that its email service had been hacked. One result was that users' email accounts were used to distribute potentially malicious spam to their contacts.

Hacks of Facebook, Twitter, and other social network accounts are not uncommon. Facebook provides an easy-to-use "My Account Is Compromised" mechanism to help members regain control if they suspect they have been hacked.

Notorious cases of cyber breaches have involved adult dating sites, too. Adult FriendFinder's user records were breached in March 2015, losing the email addresses, usernames, passwords, birthdays, and other information about more than 3 million people.

Four months later, thieves obtained records of the users of Ashley Madison, a matching website for people interested in secret relationships. A cyber gang known as the Impact Team threatened to publish the information unless the site was taken down. Their motive, the hackers claimed, was that Ashley Madison failed to provide secrecy for its members. A month later, the site was still running and the thieves released personal details of some 37 million users. Extortionists reportedly used some of the information to threaten public shaming unless targeted members paid them in Bitcoins. At least one person whose identity was exposed committed suicide. Members filed a multimillion-dollar class action lawsuit against the website owners.

In August 2014, hackers released digital photographs of hundreds of celebrities, some of them shown in embarrassing situations. The cyber attackers were able to break through the security technology of iCloud, Apple's online computing and data storage service.

INDIVIDUAL COMPUTER AND INTERNET USERS

Cyber invasions of individuals' computer systems occur daily. They can begin when someone opens an email attachment sent by a criminal in the guise of a trusted acquaintance or relative. The file may contain malicious code that infects the recipient's computer in a matter of seconds.

Mobile phones are not immune to cyber attacks, but many users seem to think they are and neglect to take precautions.

Social media sites are notorious hunting grounds for cyber criminals. Security experts caution against including information in personal profiles that might be used for identity theft. Mobile phones are especially vulnerable targets. One reason is that many people don't bother to apply anti-malware safeguards on their phones like they do on their desktop or laptop computers.

Untold sums are extracted daily from the many online accounts of unsuspecting people whose identities have been swiped. Banks and credit card companies offer account protection for their customers, but much of the stolen money never is recovered. The consequence for some victims is a ruined credit record for years to come.

CHAPTER 2

ATTACKERS HAVE THE ADVANTAGE

A cyber gang of teenagers broke into the personal AOL email account of CIA (Central Intelligence Agency) Director John Brennan in October 2015. The best encryption used on the Internet could not have prevented it. Why not? The group, calling themselves "Crackas With Attitude," simply went around the technology safeguards. They succeeded by a series of telecommunication and social engineering tricks.

First, they learned Brennan was a customer of the Verizon mobile communication service. One of the group phoned Verizon, posing as an online technician who was attempting to respond to a customer's service call. Claiming his access to the customer's account information temporarily was down, he obtained details about Brennan's Verizon account. Also, he was given information about Brennan's AOL account.

An embarrassing and alarming breach in 2015 was the temporary theft of CIA director John Brennan's AOL email account.

The gang then called AOL, pretending to have lost access to their (Brennan's) email account. Using confidential information about Brennan they had obtained from Verizon, they persuaded an AOL representative to reset the account password, believing the true account owner was on the line. For three days, they invaded Brennan's email before the breach was discovered and the account was removed. They obtained and distributed Brennan's contact list and other information, including a lengthy security document containing sensitive private data.

Understandably, Brennan was furious. According to an article by Marisa Schultz in the *New York Post,* he told reporters the incident demonstrates "just how vulnerable people are to those who want to cause harm" in the era of global connectivity on the Internet. With clever social engineering and manipulation of electronic communication systems, criminals have new techniques for carrying out attacks against society.

A British teenager was arrested in February 2016 in connection with the case. He was charged with suspicion of conspiracy and released on bail.

This penetration by juveniles of a personal phone account belonging to one of the world's highest-ranking security officials was amusing to hackers, sobering to society. It was but one of many recent high-profile government and corporate breaches. It demonstrated that in the modern age, cryptography is being combined with human cunning in the execution of cyber attacks. Defenders must take into account all the tools used by hackers. Because they always are on the offensive, hackers decidedly have the advantage.

DIFFICULTIES IN COPING WITH CYBER THREATS

One of the first tasks of authorities and IT professionals—after controlling the damage of a breach—is identifying the source of an attack. It is not always easy, because often they have few clues to go on. In some cases, they recognize likely suspects by their method and objectives, based on a pattern of previous attacks. Eventually, a cyber gang or individual may claim responsibility. Sometimes, more than one hacker professes to be the burglar, complicating the investigation.

While cyber criminals are free to perform their dirty work at an unchecked pace, governments and the administrators of businesses and industries are bogged down for months or even years developing and agreeing on measures to counteract their dangers. Legal analysts note that new laws and policies are based on events that have occurred

Not all hackers are experienced programmers. Many are teenagers and children with average computer skills.

in the past. It is not so easy to address the mischief that might be unleashed tomorrow.

The struggle is similar to a football or basketball game, except that the hackers always have the ball. Cyber defenders make the best educated guesses they can about what "play" the hackers might try next—what their next target will be and how they will attack. One cybersecurity professional has likened the task of prevention to driving backward, trying to steer via the rearview mirror.

Juveniles and adults with only modest computer skills can indulge in cybercrime. Malware programs and systems are available for purchase or rental online. It takes little time or training to learn how to become a hacker.

Until recently, it was difficult for prosecutors to convict hacker "hobbyists." Authorities needed to prove not only that the hacking tool was used inappropriately, but also that it was obtained with actual criminal intent. The novice hacker could claim it was merely an experimental or recreational exercise.

Laws against cybercrime are becoming more stringent. However, the ready availability of malware and the growing legions of hackers pose a daunting problem for law enforcement and society. Judicial system observers note that the more hackers who are brought to justice, the more choked court dockets become.

PSYCHOLOGICAL FACTORS

Hackers have a psychological advantage in knowing that even if they are caught and convicted, it's unlikely they will serve a long jail term—if any. In major incidents of economic espionage, heavy fines may be imposed on the agents who are apprehended, or caught, but they know their backers can easily pay. They soon will be back at work.

In the 1980s and 1990s, computer criminals were rarely sentenced to prison. Laws and prosecutions have become much more aggressive since the turn of the century. Still, many hackers consider the potential monetary rewards or their passion for a political or social agenda worth the risks.

The psychology on the target side of the equation also tends to work to hackers' advantage. Many business owners and individuals

gamble on the notion that criminals aren't interested in them or their digital information. Hackers, they reason, have bigger fish to fry. Consequently, they fail to effectively secure their personal and customer data. State and federal laws are requiring more rigorous efforts by businesses to protect customer data, but new regulations and guidelines are hard to

Besides the theft of personal information, victims of cyber attacks may lose dozens of hours in frustration trying to restore their computers.

THE DARK WEB

The so-called Dark Web is a segment of the Internet that is not seen by typical Internet users, because its sites are not indexed by popular search engines. The Dark Web is not altogether devious, but it worries law enforcement and security agencies because of its use by cyber criminals. Malware and services offered by hackers are often found there. Stolen credit card information is trafficked regularly on the Dark Web, a practice known as carding; so are illegal drugs, firearms, counterfeit money, and other illegal products.

In 2015, law enforcement authorities in 20 countries coordinated efforts to take down Darkode, a Dark Web forum where cyber criminals bought, sold, and rented malware and pilfered data. More than 70 Darkode participants were arrested in locations around the world. The cooperative police action was called Operation Shrouded Horizon.

The Darkode bust was a victory against cybercrime. Officials acknowledge, though, that it did little to obstruct global hacking. Dark Web entities dealing in underground data and criminal cyber tools number in the hundreds, possibly thousands.

enforce. Not until a breach has occurred are authorities likely to scrutinize a company's security policy and procedures.

In international attacks, even when the originator is identified, international laws and politics sometimes hamper prosecution. For example, the US government cannot force a suspected or known Russian hacker to be extradited to the United States for trial. Understandably, officials believe Russian nationals are among the leading hackers who target US government computers. They also are said to be at the forefront of black market contraband sales. A 2014 report submitted to the US Department of Justice was based on a study of message threads from 13 underground web forums where stolen products are advertised. While the forums were hosted in different countries, 10 of them used Russian as their primary language.

FEAR ITSELF IS A CYBER WEAPON

The very threat of a cyber breach affects the way in which corporate employees are able to do their work. A consequence of the increasing cyber attacks has been that corporations must place new restraints on their workers.

In a 2015 survey sponsored by Gemalto, a digital security company, more than 90 percent of participating information technology professionals said their IT departments prohibit company employees from exchanging sensitive company data while using their mobile phones, tablets, and laptop computers. Corporations fear that mobile data exchanges by employees while working away from their offices are unprotected by the company's internal security technology. As a result, data might be stolen with ease from an employee's mobile device. This could lead to a hack into the company's main computer system and data.

Thus, employees are hampered in their work. Amazing advances in mobile technology offer them impressive ways to share information more efficiently. However, the reality of cyber criminals lurking in the digital neighborhood limits the practical use of mobile computing. Ironically, hackers do not have to actually do anything in order to cause a certain degree of disruption.

SOBERING STATISTICS

With so many factors working in their favor, it is small wonder cyber criminals are flourishing. The Statistic Brain research project reports that more than

Some hackers accomplish their dirty work using ordinary laptop or tablet computers with malware apps bought or rented via the Dark Web.

12 million Americans are victims of identity theft each year. That represents approximately 7.5 percent of US households.

Identity theft is costly—and growing costlier. Statistic Brain shows that the total monetary loss attributed to identity theft was $13.2 billion in 2010; by 2014, it was double that amount. Most of the losses resulted from a misuse of credit cards or bank accounts. About 14 percent resulted from a misuse of personal information.

Typically, the original data thieves profit not by impersonating a victim, but by selling the stolen databank on the Dark Web. According to Holt and Smirnova, a 2014 report prepared for the National Criminal Justice Reference Service found that on the Dark Web, the average "dump" of bank account or credit card data brought the seller $102.60. The authors of the study wrote, "Recent evidence suggests that hackers who acquire sensitive consumer data sell this information to others in on-line forums for a profit. In turn, an underground economy has developed around the sale of stolen data, involving various resources that can be used to convert electronic data into real world currency and engage in various forms of cybercrime."

The tools criminals use to steal computer data have been growing exponentially. Symantec, vendor of the Norton software security suite, says 1.2 million new malware threats were created every day in 2015. To counter them, security software companies update their customers' virus definitions constantly. They urge users to download the latest antivirus definitions regularly.

CHAPTER 3

WHAT DO CYBER CRIMINALS WANT?

A US district court in May 2014 accused five Chinese military hackers of computer hacking and economic espionage, as well as about 30 connected crimes. The Federal Bureau of Investigation reported that this was the first time criminal charges had been pressed against "known state actors for hacking." The Chinese government denied involvement.

The defendants were officers in the Chinese People's Liberation Army. Their conspiracy began in 2006 and continued until about the time of their indictments. Their objectives: to obtain nuclear power plant blueprints, steel factory computer data, and solar energy company information. Specific targets were Westinghouse Electric; American subsidiaries of Solar-World AG; United States Steel; Allegheny Technologies; the United Steel, Paper and Forestry, Rubber, Manufacturing, Energy, Allied Industrial and Service Workers International Union; and Alcoa.

In a Federal Bureau of Investigation press release, US Attorney General Eric Holder, remarked, "The range of trade secrets and other sensitive business information stolen in this case is significant and demands an aggressive response. Success in the global market place should be based solely on a company's ability to innovate and compete, not on a sponsor government's ability to spy and steal business secrets."

John Carlin, assistant attorney general for national security, added, "State actors engaged in cyber espionage for economic advantage are not immune from the law just because they hack under the shadow of their country's flag. Cyber theft is real theft, and we will hold state-sponsored cyber thieves accountable as we would any other transnational criminal organization that steals our goods and breaks our laws."

A cybersecurity expert, Thomas Brown, told a CNN reporter, "The Chinese are going after every single economic advantage they can obtain. Decades of time spent developing technologies are being ripped off and stolen every day." Security observers explain that American companies spend millions of dollars in trial-and-error research to perfect a new technology or product. Foreign governments who manage to steal the intelligence spend nothing on research; they simply duplicate the final product.

Cyber attacks are often "fishing expeditions." The hackers are not sure of the exact nature of the data they will find. They simply extract large volumes of information, then analyze it to learn what, if anything, they can use for profit. They may find, for instance, email

Eric Holder, former US attorney general, advocated an aggressive response to cybercrimes perpetrated to obtain international trade secrets.

addresses and other information about government officials or professionals in high-level positions. Using this personal information, they might pose as the professional to obtain confidential data from colleagues or to conduct illegal financial transactions.

Other attacks are against specific targets with specific objectives. Some cyber thieves are after a particular type of information. Government-backed hackers primarily seek classified information from other governments. In the case above, the defendants sought classified information about US government contractors.

Different hackers want information of different types for different reasons. They select their victims accordingly.

Hacking the World of Finance

Money is the ultimate prize for many cyber criminals. While credit card theft can bring immediate rewards, larger plots are devised to acquire much greater wealth in roundabout ways.

The theft of massive stores of data from JPMorgan Chase in 2014 was effected by foreign hackers.

An attack on JPMorgan Chase in 2014 extracted data linked to more than 80 million bank accounts. It is believed to be the largest data theft ever conducted against a US banking institution and its customers. Police in November 2015 arrested three men, including two Israelis, in connection with the JPMorgan Chase heist and hacks of other financial firms. They were charged with hacking and attempting to hack computers and with securities fraud.

The hackers reportedly used the stolen data in various financial schemes. One involved manipulating stock prices. They also allegedly laundered money for criminals and also ran illegal online gambling operations.

The investigation took more than a year and was conducted by authorities in 11 countries. They eventually learned that the JPMorgan Chase breach was conducted from an Egyptian computer system.

In the summer of 2015, hackers obtained data from the computers of several major law firms that represent leading American banks and corporations. Investigators believe the motive for the breaches may have been to obtain private financial information. Ultimately, the data could be used for insider trading.

That case demonstrated that when in quest of confidential information concerning finances, hackers may not go after financial institutions directly. Here, they obtained what they wanted with an indirect tactic. Some law firm databases contain, for example, details about clients' patent applications or merger negotiations. This information, if made public, could be valuable to investors making stock purchases.

Such attacks are not focused on large law firms alone. Hackers understand that smaller firms storing sensitive information may have less robust computer security systems.

A particular cause of alarm is the time it takes for information technology staffs to realize a breach has occurred. By the time of discovery, sensitive information may have passed through many networks online. Cyber criminals have warned that they plan more elaborate and more damaging attacks.

CYBER RANSOMING AND BLACKMAIL

The crime of ransom has been performed for many centuries. It is a basic criminal technique. A lone criminal or group of people steal something— not because of its monetary value, but because of its greater value to the victim. The thief offers to return it for a lot of money, a ransom.

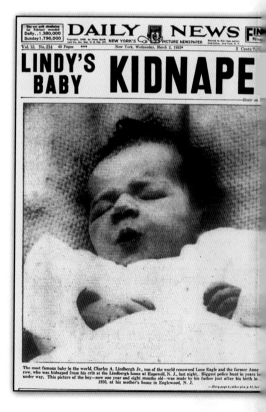

The Lindbergh kidnapping/ransom case in 1932 ended in tragedy. By contrast, cyber criminals usually release confiscated data after the ransom is paid.

One of the most infamous ransom cases was the Lindbergh kidnapping in 1932. Someone stole by night into the estate of famous aviator Charles Lindbergh and took away his 19-month-old son. The kidnapper left a note demanding $50,000 for the safe return of the toddler. The ransom money was paid, but the boy was not returned. A month later, his body was discovered.

This event was typical of traditional ransom cases. Police know that rarely is a kidnapped person released unharmed after a ransom is paid. The criminals take the money, murder the victim, and run. They reason that, if freed, the kidnapped person could provide police with clues as to their identity.

In the twenty-first century, most ransom cases are occurring on the Internet or with digital data. They do not involve human hostages or collectible treasures. They involve information and information systems. Criminal software engineers have developed a category of malware to carry out cyber ransoming. Security experts refer to it as ransomware.

The first case of cyber ransom occurred in 1989. During the next decade, ransomware made its way onto individuals' personal computers.

Ron Young, the police chief in Damariscotta, Maine, reported that his department was forced to pay a ransom to cyber criminals.

CRASHING WEBSITES

Cyber criminals frequently disrupt the websites of government agencies, companies, banks, and individuals with denial-of-service (DoS) attacks. Essentially, they bombard the web server with requests that either overwhelm or crash the site. The result is that customers or legitimate visitors are unable to access the site. Criminals' motives may be sabotage, militant activism, or blackmail. DoS techniques are varied. Typically, a flood of hits to the site comes from thousands of outside computer addresses. Another form of DoS is dubbed a "banana" program. It is able to bounce messages sent from the targeted site back to the site.

Simply described, virus code locks data files stored on the computer. Only the criminal has the key that will unlock it. Instructions are displayed on the owner's computer, declaring that to regain the data, money must be paid into an online account in the form of Bitcoin, which cannot be traced to the recipient.

Cyber ransoming continues to be inflicted on individuals, but criminals find it more lucrative to target businesses and organizations. Symantec, a computer security software vendor, has reported that ransomware occurrences multiplied from 100,000 to 600,000 between January and December 2013.

Interestingly, in modern scenarios, online criminals usually do what they promise to do once they receive the money. It is to their future benefit to conduct business in this "honorable" way. Cybercrime analysts, however, caution victims to bear in mind that any ransom they pay often goes to crime syndicates and, in some cases, to terrorist organizations.

Ransomware is not the only means by which criminals extract payment from computer users. In some cases, they simply resort to old-fashioned blackmail. They obtain sensitive information or compromising images of an individual. They threaten to distribute the damaging material unless a fee is paid.

SABOTAGE AND TERRORISM

Financial gain is not the only motive underlying cybercrime. Some hackers, bent on promoting political and social agendas, attempt to wound or destroy organizations and societies they consider enemies. Others are cyber vandals, out to cause random damage to as many people as they can.

Computers are sabotaged by viruses and other malware. Generally, the harmful programs are spread by email. When an unsuspecting recipient opens an attached file, an embedded malware program is executed on the recipient's computer.

Viruses can ruin a computer in different ways. Some delete or alter the victim's files. Others duplicate themselves thousands of times, occupying all of the storage space on the hard drive. Some are simply hoaxes, causing no real harm, but popping up whimsical or sarcastic messages on the screen.

Other types of malware used for computer sabotage are worms, Trojan horses, and logic bombs. Worms are able to replicate themselves using the computer operating system, without the user opening a poisoned file attachment. A common symptom is a steady slowing of the computer's performance, often resulting in a system crash.

A Trojan horse is a computer game or utility that appears to be enjoyable or useful. When installed, it may do what the victim expects it to do—but in the background, it is causing damage. Some are programmed to delete data. Others send information to the Trojan horse creator about the victim's computer or allow the creator to install cookies.

A logic bomb is malware that, when installed, resides dormant for a period of time. It does not activate until a specified date or until the victim performs a certain action at the keyboard.

Terrorists use malware to damage corporate or government computer systems. In addition to disrupting operations and extracting data, they seek to gain control for malicious purposes. Security experts note, for example, that if hackers are able to manipulate a factory's computers, they conceivably could control machinery, wreaking havoc on production processes.

1010100111001101101 100 110110 1100 0110110011010
200 101110001101011110011101 010110011011010011101
10 01011 0101100 0110 11101110110110100101100 00101
101 011001101101001111010 10 01 110 1 010
011 101 101 110 1011 1001 11 01 0111
11 01 01
11 110
01 1 0
01 110
10

CHAPTER 4

THE NATIONS RESPOND

N ations and companies are groping for the best solutions and defenses against the threat. A complication is that cyber attacks sometimes overlap between national crimes and international espionage. Investigating a breach of a company in one country by hackers in another can be a

delicate matter. It requires cooperation between the nations, sometimes bringing international politics into play.

In the United States, the Computer Fraud and Abuse Act of 1986 has been a fundamental federal law that criminalizes cybercrime activities. It addresses crimes that affect government computers or those of financial institutions that might disrupt the economy. It also deals with crimes involving DoS attacks and the spreading of malicious code. The act has been revised many times.

Other federal laws often come into play. Notable is RICO, the Racketeer

President Barack Obama in 2015 threatened economic sanctions against foreign perpetrators of cyber espionage against the United States.

Influenced and Corrupt Organizations Act. It basically deals with organized crime, which now encompasses financial hacking. Additionally, states have passed legislation aimed at controlling the cybercrime plague. While enacting laws for punishing the criminals, they also are requiring corporations and organizations—particularly credit card companies—to better secure their customers' and clients' personal information.

President Barack Obama issued an executive order in April 2015 creating economic sanctions against persons or entities overseas who are proven responsible for cyber attacks that threaten the nation's security, financial institutions, economic stability, or foreign policies. In effect, the US Treasury can freeze violators' financial resources. The executive order says such an attack constitutes a national emergency. The Obama administration acknowledged that cyber threats are growing.

The Cybersecurity Information Sharing Act (CISA) was signed into law in the United States in December 2015. It calls for government agencies, private companies, and other organizations to share information that might provide warning clues to cybercrime threats. Theoretically, by sharing alerts and other information, all the entities will be able to protect their data more effectively.

However, many information technology analysts have criticized the act. They claim it will have limited effect as an anti-espionage measure. Sharing past information, they point out, will not necessarily prevent terrorists' current and future plots.

At the same time, privacy advocates are worried that the act will violate individuals' rights. Personal information about innocent people might be circulated among government and private data gatherers.

TOUGH NEW LAWS IN EUROPE

The European Union (EU) in 2013 issued a directive concerning attacks against information systems. Its objective is "to tackle large-scale cyber-attacks by requiring EU Member States to strengthen national cyber-crime laws and introduce tougher criminal sanctions."

Also in 2013, the European Cybercrime Centre (EC3), developed by the European Commission, began operations. Its stated goal: "EC3 acts as the focal point in the fight against cybercrime in the Union, pooling European cybercrime expertise to support Member States' cybercrime investigations and providing a collective voice of European cybercrime investigators across law enforcement and the judiciary."

In the United Kingdom, the Serious Crime Act 2015 passed by Parliament went into effect. It included tougher cybercrime measures, amending the country's Computer Misuse Act 1990 "to ensure sentences for attacks on computer systems fully reflect the damage they cause." An unauthorized act of computer misuse that seriously damages a nation's economy or environment could bring a prison sentence of up to 14 years. If the misuse results in serious damage to national security or human life, the penalty could be life imprisonment.

The act tightened the legal terminology dealing with the exchange of hacker tools (malware). It also broadened the reach of law enforcement and judicial authorities, allowing them to prosecute UK citizens who commit a computer crime outside the country.

While countries around the world are strengthening cybercrime laws, law enforcement agencies are sharing information and working together. International cybercrime stings are becoming more frequent. In June

2015, for example, a joint operation by Europol and agencies in Ukraine, Estonia, Latvia, and other countries cracked a Ukrainian ring suspected of distributing two Trojan strains, ZeuS and SpyEye. "The cybercriminals used malware to attack online banking systems in Europe and beyond, adapting their sophisticated banking Trojans over time to defeat the security measures implemented by the banks," Europol announced. The group sold their technology to various cyber criminals via the Internet. Police arrested five suspects and seized computers in different locations throughout Ukraine.

HACKERS FACE LONGER JAIL SENTENCES

In the 1980s, when personal computers and the Internet were young, hacking events were not nearly as sophisticated or damaging as they are now. Arrests were comparatively few. When convicted, hackers typically were given merely a judicial "slap on the wrist"—perhaps a few months of probation and an order to repay any financial losses a victim could prove.

Cybercrime today is a much greater threat to society. Laws and punishments have become more severe. Here are examples of recent cases:

- In 2014, David Ray Camez was sentenced to 20 years in prison on racketeering charges. Camez was a leader of carder.su, a website whose operatives sold stolen identity and credit information about millions of consumers. He also was ordered to pay a share of restitution to victims.

- Albert Gonzalez was sentenced to 20 years in 2010 for stealing customer information from companies including TJX, Barnes & Noble, and Office Max. Gonzalez reportedly was the mastermind behind the theft and reselling of millions of credit and debit card numbers. One accomplice, Christopher Scott, was sentenced to seven years.
- Two Romanians, Adrian-Tiberiu Oprea and Iulian Dolan, pled guilty in 2013 to hacking the point-of-sale payment systems of multiple US restaurants and other merchants. They obtained credit and debit card details of more than 100,000 retail customers. One of the codefendants was sentenced to 15 years, the other to seven years.
- In 2015, Hieu Minh Ngo, a Vietnamese citizen, was sentenced to 13 years in prison for stealing the IDs of more than 200 million Americans. By selling the data to other cyber criminals, he profited in the amount of approximately $2 million.
- Nichole Michelle Merzi and her companion Kenneth Lucas II in 2011 were sentenced to five and eleven years, respectively, for their leadership roles in Operation Phish Phry. Their group intercepted account information belonging to Bank of America and Wells Fargo customers. The international gang included more than 100 members; some of the others also were convicted and received lesser sentences. The breakup of the gang resulted after several years of investigation by American and Egyptian authorities.
- Jeremy Hammond, a member of Anonymous who dubbed himself "Anarchaos," was handed a 10-year prison term in 2013. Hammond was involved in the hacking of Strategic Forecasting (Stratfor), a global intelligence firm. The FBI said he and his

confederates stole Stratfor employees' email addresses as well as information from the accounts of some 860,000 company clients.

How Harsh Should Punishment Be?

Journalists, legislators, and judicial analysts in recent years have engaged in a spirited debate over cybercrime laws and court sentences. Practically all agree with the age-old principle that "the punishment should fit the crime." They disagree sharply, though, as to what constitutes an appropriate fit. Some would be much more lenient than others.

Computer and Internet crimes vary greatly, from domestic harassment to identity theft to government-level breaches. Penalties vary likewise. For lesser offenses, a hacker might merely be sentenced to a short period of probation. Fines on these crimes can range from a few hundred dollars for minor incidents to hundreds of thousands of dollars for cybercrimes ruled to be felonies. Jail time may be as short as several months or longer than 20 years.

Christopher Chaney in 2012 was sentenced to 10 years for posting online nude photographs of actresses whose email accounts he had infiltrated. He ultimately admitted his actions were terrible violations of privacy.

Some criminal justice analysts have applauded more severe punishment in recent years. They are joined by victims of cybercrimes who have suffered greatly from money and time losses. Some observers, however, are more sympathetic to cyber criminals. They don't believe hacking is at the same level of wrongdoing as, for example, criminal violence. They even contend that some cyber breaches are for the common good. That is, hackers might be breaking into classified databases that contain certain government or academic records that, in their view, ought to be available to the public.

Technology columnist Roger Grimes wrote in a 2013 *InfoWorld* article, "I'm no friend of the malicious hacker. I think all unauthorized significant and malicious computer activity should be punished ... But perhaps malicious hackers should serve fewer years in prison than convicted murderers."

A complication is the difficulty of calculating how much damage a cyber attack causes. Hackers who plant a DoS utility in a business website undoubtedly inflict a loss in sales to online customers—but how much of a loss? How many frustrated customers are turned away? How much money would they have spent? The victims, lawyers, judges, and juries can only speculate.

Victims of computer viruses have had to spend dozens, even hundreds, of hours restoring their computers to normal operations. Few keep track of the time. Even if they did, what dollar value could be placed on their time loss? How can authorities accurately determine how many people are affected by a particular virus?

A further dilemma is that cybercrimes often are not discovered until months or years after they take place. By then, any attempt to calculate the extent of damage, or even make a reasonable estimate, is virtually impossible.

Needed: A Strategy for Countering Cybercrime

In 2014, researchers Thomas J. Holt of Michigan State University and Olga Smirnova of East Carolina University presented a report to the National Criminal Justice Reference Service. Titled "Examining the Structure, Organization, and Process of the International Market for Stolen Data," their study was conducted with funding by the US Department of Justice. The authors sampled almost 2,000 communication threads from web forums through which buyers and sellers advertise stolen data and other products. They concluded that "the market for stolen data is a real threat to consumers and businesses alike."

An automated popup, such as the one pictured here, alerts the user that this computer has been compromised by a virus.

COLLABORATION IS THE KEY

The FBI and other agencies stand ready to assist companies that find themselves targets of economic espionage. In many cases, they have been able to work in cooperation with victims to track and apprehend the criminals. A difficulty in some situations is that employees of targeted businesses and industries are wary of becoming involved, fearing they may be endangering themselves.

The Company Man: Protecting America's Secrets is an FBI-produced movie based on a real-life event. In that case, Chinese operatives used spy technology to glean details about an American manufacturing company in an attempt to duplicate its production secrets. When a company engineer reported to authorities that he had been approached and offered a bribe to work illicitly with the foreign agents, the FBI set up a sting operation. It resulted in the arrest and conviction of two Chinese agents for the theft of trade secrets.

The FBI posts updates on successful cybercrime prosecutions. It also maintains a "Cyber's Most Wanted" web page (www.fbi.gov/wanted/cyber).

Holt and Smirnova suggested several countermeasures against cyber criminals. One tactic is to strike at the payment systems used by the data thieves. Authorities also could go undercover to establish black market forums and in that way build cases against participating criminal networks.

The authors further cited a need for increased funding for agencies including the FBI, Secret Service, Department of Homeland Security, and Treasury

次中美打击网络犯罪及相关事项高级别联合对

cond U.S.-China High-Level Joint Dialogue on Cybercrime and Related I

2016年6月14日 中国·北京　　　　　June 14, 2016　Beijing, China

Diplomats from the United States and China met in 2016 for a high-level conference to discuss international issues related to cybercrime.

ME? A CYBER ATTACK VICTIM?

Regrettably, millions of individuals who use the Internet are all-too-easy targets for cyber criminals who would use their records for malicious purposes. Throughout each day, they post messages, videos of themselves and friends, and personal details on social media where their flimsy passwords permit easy intrusion. Their smart phones and tablet PCs keep them constantly online, in contact with the world at large.

That world at large is not altogether friendly. A teen who goes online for gaming, entertainment streaming, and communicating with friends is a potential target of cyber criminals. Her or his identity—complete with personal videos, close-up photographs, and comments lifted from Facebook or Twitter posts—can be misconstrued and misrepresented to the world by an impostor.

Young people using mobile devices are little different from bank managers and government administrators working from office computers, in the minds of cyber criminals. They, too, must take safeguards to protect themselves—and those linked to them—from online malice.

Department. The funds would be used "to increase the technological, investigative, and support resources within federal law enforcement agencies. This includes linguists and translators who understand both technical language and the jargon and slang common to market actors."

The report urged improved cooperation between law enforcement and security agencies internationally. It also recommended more research into the "organizational and economic impact of stolen data markets."

At the domestic level, Holt and Smirnova suggested public awareness campaigns to heighten consumer awareness of cybercrime and safety measures that individuals should take. They pointed out "a need for improved awareness of the risks of electronic identity theft among home computer users who do not necessarily have a strong grasp of basic computer security principles."

To malware programmers engaged in cybercrime, what they do is not unlike what millions of skilled computer gaming enthusiasts around the world do every day. They are assigned a mission. With dazzling computer skill and savvy, they carry out their assignments of devising new ways to cause mischief and mayhem, using the Internet as their vehicle.

To cryptography experts working on the Internet, what they do is much the same. They are assigned the mission of detecting, identifying, and thwarting the formidable array of digital aggressors. They use many of the same techno-tools in their work. Only occasionally can they get ahead of the criminals, whose next moves are unknown. Their objectives are to prevent breaches as best they can, control the damage when hacks occur, and apprehend the miscreants.

GLOSSARY

Bitcoin A direct, person-to-person payment system via the Internet, which cyber criminals use for such purposes as extortion and ransom transactions.

breach The process of breaking or ignoring a law or agreement.

class action A lawsuit filed on behalf of a group of plaintiffs.

classified Refers to information that is kept secret from the public by a government agency or business.

cookie A utility file automatically installed on an Internet user's computer that regularly sends information to the cookie owner about the user's online activities.

decipher To decode enciphered data.

digital Referring to information in the form of binary digits, for use with computers.

docket A list of pending court cases.

encipher To encode a message or data collection.

espionage The act of spying, often by governments, to gather information of a political or military nature.

executive order A special regulation or legal interpretation issued by the president without congressional approval.

extortionist A criminal who gets money from a victim by intimidation, threatening to reveal embarrassing or incriminating information if money is not paid.

extradite To deliver a criminal or suspect from authorities in one state to authorities in another state or from one country to another.

felony A form of "high crime," more serious than a misdemeanor.

firewall Computer software or hardware that prevents unauthorized access to the owner's data.

heirloom A family treasure handed down from generation to generation.

indictment A formal written accusation issued by a prosecuting agency against a criminal suspect.

launder To handle money illegally, disguising its source.

meatspace The real, or physical, world, as opposed to the virtual world or cyberspace.

probation A period of supervised conduct imposed on a convicted criminal, rather than a fine or confinement.

restitution Court-ordered return of stolen goods or payment of their monetary value by a convicted criminal to the victim.

sanctions The withholding of economic or other privileges by one or more countries against another country that has committed a breach of international law or accepted international behavior.

server The primary computer in a network that manages and routes program tools and data files for other computers connected to the network.

social engineering Gaining a computer user's confidence; various social engineering tactics are used legally by Internet marketers and illegally by cyber criminals.

sting A confidence plot used by law enforcement authorities against criminals to obtain clear evidence of illegal activity.

telecommunication Communication, usually long-distance, by phone or Internet.

FOR MORE INFORMATION

Computer Crime and Intellectual Property Section (CCIPS)
US Department of Justice
10th Street and Constitution Avenue NW
John C. Keeney Building, Suite 600
Washington, DC 20530
(202) 514-1026
Website: https://www.justice.gov/criminal-ccips
The CCIPS implements the US Department of Justice's strategies against
    international computer and intellectual property crimes.

Cyber Security Program
York University, School of Continuing Studies
4700 Keele Street
Toronto, ON M3J 1P3
Canada
(416) 736-5616
Website: http://continue.yorku.ca/certificates/certificate-in-cyber-security
The Cyber Security Program prepares students to lead teams and projects
    in information security management. It was developed in response to
    employers' growing need for qualified information security professionals.

European Cybercrime Centre (EC3)
Europol
PO Box 908 50
2509 LW The Hague

The Netherlands
+ 31 70 302 5000
Website: https://www.europol.europa.eu/ec3
Part of Europol, the European Cybercrime Centre began operations in
    January 2013. Its purpose is to strengthen the law enforcement
    response to cybercrime in the European Union and to help protect
    European citizens, businesses, and governments.

Federal Bureau of Investigation
    J. Edgar Hoover Building
        935 Pennsylvania Avenue NW
        Washington, DC 20535-0001
        (202) 324-3000
            Website: http://www.fbi.gov
            The bureau's website contains details about how the FBI works to
            combat cybercrime.

Interpol
    General Secretariat
        200 quai Charles de Gaulle
        69006 Lyon
        France
        Fax: +33 (0)4 72 44 71 63
            Website: http://www.interpol.int/Crime-areas/Cybercrime/
            Cybercrime
            Interpol is the world's largest international police organi-
            zation. It has 190 member nations. More and more of its
            work involves cybercrime.

        Royal Canadian Mounted Police
            Headquarters Building

73 Leikin Drive
Ottawa, ON K1A 0R2
Canada
(613) 993-7267
Website: http://www.rcmp-grc.gc.ca
Canada's historic crime fighting organization today is engaged in battling
    cybercrime as well as traditional criminal activities.

US Computer Emergency Readiness Team (US-CERT)
US Department of Homeland Security
245 Murray Lane SW, Building 410
Washington, DC 20598
(888) 282-0870
Website: https://www.dhs.gov
The Department of Homeland Security is one of several federal
    agencies working to foil cybercrime and cyber terrorism.
    US-CERT is the departmental branch that specializes in
    defending against cyber attacks.

WEBSITES

Because of the changing nature of Internet links, Rosen
Publishing has developed an online list of websites related
to the subject of this book. This site is updated regularly.
Please use this link to access the list:

http://www.rosenlinks.com/CCMBC/attack

FOR FURTHER READING

Bailey, Diane. *Cyber Ethics* (Cyber Citizenship and Cyber Safety). New York, NY: Rosen Central, 2008.

Curley, Rob, ed. *Cryptography: Cracking Codes* (Intelligence and Counterintelligence). New York, NY: Rosen Education Service, 2013.

Day-MacLeod, Deirdre. *Viruses and Spam* (Cyber Citizenship and Cyber Safety). New York, NY: Rosen Central, 2008.

Gitlin, Martin, and Margaret J. Goldstein. *Cyber Security*. Minneapolis, MN: Twenty-First Century Books, 2015.

Gray, Leon. *Cybercrime* (Crime Science). New York, NY: Gareth Stevens Publishing, 2013.

Grayson, Robert. *The FBI and Cyber Crime* (The FBI Story). Broomall, PA: Mason Crest, 2014.

Hile, Kevin. *Cybercrime* (Crime Scene Investigations). San Diego, CA: Lucent Books, 2010.

Hynson, Colin. *Cyber Crime* (Inside Crime). Mankato, MN: Smart Apple Media, 2011.

Latta, Sara L. *Cybercrime: Data Trails Do Tell Tales* (True Forensic Crime Stories). New York, NY: Enslow Publishing, 2011.

MacIntosh, Neil. *Cyber Crime* (Face the Facts). Portsmouth, NH: Heinemann Publishing, 2003.

Mitra, Ananda. *Digital Security: Cyber Terror and Cyber Security* (Digital World). New York, NY: Chelsea House Publications, 2010.

Orr, Tamra. *Privacy and Hacking* (Cyber Citizenship and Cyber Safety). New York, NY: Rosen Central, 2008.

Rich, Mari. *Cyber Spy Hunters!* (Scientists in Action). Broomall, PA: Mason Crest, 2015.

Rooney, Anne. *Computer Science and IT: Investigating a Cyber Attack* (Anatomy of an Investigation). Portsmouth, NH: Heinemann Publishing, 2013.

Ross, Jeffrey Ian. *Cybercrime* (Criminal Investigations). New York, NY: Chelsea House Publications, 2009.

Stefoff, Rebecca. *Cyber Crime* (Forensic Science Investigated). New York, NY: Cavendish Square Publishing, 2008.

Townsend, John. *Cyber Crime* (Raintree Freestyle). Portsmouth, NH: Heinemann Publishing, 2004.

Townsend, John. *Cyber Crime Secrets* (Amazing Crime Scene Science). Mankato, MN: Amicus, 2011.

BIBLIOGRAPHY

Carte, Brian. "AOL Confirms Mail Service Hacked." *USA Today*, April 22, 2014
(www.usatoday.com/story/tech/2014/04/22/aol-email-hacked/8003859).

Cobb, Stephen. "Cybercrime Update: Take Downs, Arrests, Convictions, and
Sentences." WeLivesSecurity, July 27, 2015 (www.welivesecurity
.com/2015/07/27/cybercrime-take-downs-arrests-convictions-sentences).

The Company Man: Protecting America's Secrets. Washington, DC: Federal
Bureau of Investigation Counterintelligence Division, 2015. Retrieved April
2016 (www.fbi.gov/news/stories/2015/july/economic-espionage/video
/the-company-man-protecting-americas-secrets).

"Fear of Data Breaches Poses Obstacles to User Mobility." *The Lawyer's PC*,
December 15, 2015.

"Five Chinese Military Hackers Charged With Cyber Espionage Against U.S."
Federal Bureau of Investigation press release, May 19, 2014 (https://www
.fbi.gov/news/news_blog/five-chinese-military-hackers-charged-with
-cyber-espionage-against-u.s).

Grimes, Roger A. "Cyber Crime Sentencing Is Out of Whack." *InfoWorld*,
January 29, 2013 (www.infoworld.com/article/2613374/security/cyber
-crime-sentencing-is-out-of-whack.html).

Holt, Thomas J., and Olga Smirnova. "Examining the Structure, Organization,
and Process of the International Market for Stolen Data." National Criminal
Justice Reference Service, 2014. Retrieved April 2016 (www.ncjrs.gov
/pdffiles1/nij/grants/245375.pdf).

"Identity Theft/Fraud Statistics." Statistical Brain Research Institute, 2016.
Retrieved April 2016 (www.statisticbrain.com/identity-theft-fraud
-statistics).

Jeffreys-Jones, Rhodri. *In Spies We Trust: The Story of Western Intelligence.* Oxford, UK: Oxford University Press, 2013.

Mastroianni, Brian. "Dangerous Escalation in Ransomware Attacks." CBS News, February 19, 2016 (www.cbsnews.com/news/ransomware-hollywood-presbyterian-hospital-hacked-for-ransom).

Nakashima, Ellen. "U.S. Establishes Sanctions Program to Combat Cyberattacks, Cyberspying." *The Washington Post,* April 2, 2015 (www.washingtonpost.com/world/national-security/us-to-establish-sanctions-program-to-combat-cyberattacks-cyberspying/2015/03/31/7f563474-d7dc-11e4-ba28-f2a685dc7f89_story.html).

Osborne, Charlie. "Europol Tackles ZeuS, SpyEye Banking Trojan Cybercrime Ring." ZDNet, June 30, 2015 (www.zdnet.com/article/europol-tackles-zeus-spyeye-banking-trojan-cybercrime-ring/#!).

Pagliery, Jose. "EBay Customers Must Reset Passwords After Major Hack." CNN Money, May 21, 2016 (http://money.cnn.com/2014/05/21/technology/security/ebay-passwords/index.html).

Pagliery, Jose. "Police Bust Huge Hacker Black Market." CNN Money, July 15, 2015 (http://money.cnn.com/2015/07/15/technology/darkode-shutdown).

Pagliery, Jose. "What Were China's Hacker Spies After?" CNN Money, May 19, 2014 (http://money.cnn.com/2014/05/19/technology/security/china-hackers/?iid=EL).

Pauli, Darren. "Blighty Cops Nab Brit Teen for 'Hacking' CIA Brennan's AOL Account." *The Register,* February 15, 2016 (www.theregister.co.uk/2016/02/15/blighty_nabs_teen_brit_twit_for_hacking_cia_brennans_aol_account).

Riley, Charles. "Hackers Threaten to Release Names From Adultery Website." CNN Money, July 20, 2015 (http://money.cnn.com/2015/07/20/technology/ashley-madison-hack/index.html).

Riley, Charles. "Insurance Giant Anthem Hit by Massive Data Breach." CNN Money, February 6, 2015 (http://money.cnn.com/2015/02/04/technology/anthem-insurance-hack-data-security).

Riley, Michael, and Jordan Robertson. "Chinese State-Sponsored Hackers Suspected in Anthem Attack." BloombergTechnology, February 5, 2015 (www.bloomberg.com/news/articles/2015-02-05/signs-of-china-sponsored-hackers-seen-in-anthem-attack).

Ross, Barbara, and Dareh Gregorian. "Two Israelis, 1 American Charged in Massive Hack of JP Morgan Chase Records, Other Cyber Crimes." *New York Daily News*, November 10, 2015 (www.nydailynews.com/news/national/3-charged-massive-jp-morgan-chase-hack-article-1.2429959).

Schultz, Marisa. "CIA Director Fumes Over Teen Who Hacked Personal Email." *New York Post*, October 27, 2015 (http://nypost.com/2015/10/27/cia-director-outraged-with-teenager-who-hacked-him).

Sonowane, Vishakha. "Law Firms Cravath Swaine & Moore, Weil Gotshal & Manges, Among Others, Hacked." *International Business Times*, March 30, 2016 (www.ibtimes.com/law-firms-cravath-swaine-moore-weil-gotshal-manges-among-others-hacked-report-2345300).

Storm, Darlene. "List of Hacked Government Agencies Grows: State Department, White House, NOAA & USPS." *Computerworld*, November 17, 2014 (www.computerworld.com/article/2848779/list-of-hacked

-government-agencies-grows-state-department-white-house-noaa
-and-usps.html).

Szoldra, Paul. "The 9 Worst Cyber Attacks of 2015." Tech Insider, December 29, 2015 (www.techinsider.io/cyberattacks-2015-12).

Townsend, Kevin. "Cybercrime and Punishment." *Infosecurity Magazine*, September 2, 2014 (www.infosecurity-magazine.com/magazine -features/cybercrime-and-punishment).

Walker, Danielle. "Black Market 'Darkode' Bust Leads to Arrests in 20 Countries." *SC Magazine*, July 15, 2015 (www.scmagazine.com /international-law-enforcement-efforts-against-darkode-yields -indictments/article/426632).

Wall, Caroline. "Hackers in Chains: Class of 2015." FierceITSecurity, August 11, 2015 (www.fierceitsecurity.com/story/hackers -chains-class-2015/2015-08-11).

Wall, Caroline. "Hackers in Chains: 13 of the Biggest US Prison Sentences for Electronic Crime." FierceITSecurity, May 21, 2014 (www.fierceitsecurity.com/story/hackers-chains-13-biggest -us-prison-sentences-electronic-crime/2014-05-21).

Zetter, Kim. "Teen Who Hacked CIA Director's Email Tells How He Did It." *Wired*, October 19, 2015 (www.wired.com /2015/10/hacker-who-broke-into-cia-director-john -brennan-email-tells-how-he-did-it).

INDEX

About the Author

Daniel E. Harmon is the author of more than one hundred books including works on the FBI, military intelligence, and Internet security. He edits a legal technology newsletter, *The Lawyer's PC*, and has written thousands of articles for magazines and newspapers. A former security officer, he has a special interest in criminology. In his spare time, he writes historical crime fiction.

Photo Credits